DICE

DECEPTION, FATE & ROTTEN LUCK

RICKY JAY

Photography by

ROSAMOND PURCELL

THE QUANTUCK LANE PRESS

For Persi Diaconis, Steve Freeman & Michael Weber

R J

In memory of Stephen Jay Gould:
collaborator, dear friend, professor of contingency

R P

CONTENTS

DICE IN A BOTTLE

In 1984 a small pewter container was found embedded in silt on the North bank of the Thames near London Bridge. It was located by a metal detector wielded by a modern "mudlark," a slang term first defined by the eccentric eighteenth-century lexicographer Francis Gross as a fellow who scoured the waterside for trinkets. In 1796 the police chronicler Patrick Colquhoun imputed a criminal conspiracy between the mudlarks who searched for bankside prizes and the ship stevedores who knowingly jettisoned such cargo for a subsequent share of the profits. Today the

Society of Thames Mudlarks is a respected organization licensed by the Port of London Authority. This group has retrieved many thousands of items, ranging from belt buckles and coins to a seventeenth-century royal ring.

The receptacle unearthed from the silt was emblazoned with a double-headed eagle set within a shield. Antiquaries concluded that it was a feeding trough from a late-fifteenth-century bird cage. Instead of holding leguminous seeds as earlier specimens had, this particular model contained twenty-four small bone dice. Whether the trough was used as a cup or box from which the dice were thrown has not been determined. That the dice were the kit of a hustler was confirmed, as every die was constructed or modified for cheating.

X-ray photographs revealed that eighteen dice were all drilled out and weighted with quicksilver. Shakespeare would have called these loaded dice fulhams, named for the Thames-side community which was then rumored to be the seat of a brisk trade in illicit dicing. Eleven of the dice were set to favor fives and sixes, and these were neatly injected with three small veins of mercury; the others were infused with two veins and favored the ace and deuce.

The remaining six cubes were misspotted. Three of them, called "high men," were marked only with the numbers four, five, and six repeated (no more than three surfaces of a die are visible at one time). The others, "low men," had only one, two, or three spots indicated.

The trough was squeezed shut to make an airtight seal, after which a hustler in jeopardy likely pitched it into the Thames to thwart detection. The vessel and the dice are housed at the Museum of London.

DIGGING FOR DICE

AMID THE DETRITUS, under the mounds of ash, soot, and dirt excavated at Pompeii and Herculaneum, were found — dice. The two major gambling histories published in the nineteenth century claim that these dice were "loaded," weighted to make certain numbers appear more frequently than chance or statistics dictate. Yet, among scores of classical citations, neither book gives a specific source for this information. One study reports that the dice were found at Pompeii, the other Herculaneum. The tale is repeated in many other works, but none gives a credible provenance for the doctored dice.

In an inscription found in Pompeii a gamester congratulates himself for winning money without deception, but my efforts to find specific mention of fraudulent dice in an inventory of recovered objects, to read in the archeological record their exact size and shape, have proven futile. Were they crafted of bone or wood or ivory? Were the loads made of lead or gold or quicksilver? Who found them? Was it a dice player or an archeologist—or a dice-playing archeologist—who detected their unnatural bias?

Even if the story is apocryphal, even if the dice found in Pompeii and Herculaneum were not loaded, those used by avid Roman gamblers contained a built-in potential for cheating. In an age long before the invention of the micrometer, how could the cubes be perfectly square? Casinos now demand a product machined to within one ten-thousandth of an inch on each side. The natural imperfections of dice fashioned by hand might have been used to advantage by ancient gamesters whose empirical knowledge of percentages can be conjectured.

That the Romans were fond of dice is well known: Augustus, Domitian, Commodus, Caligula, and Nero were all inveterate players. Claudius, a flamboyant gambler, authored a treatise, "How to Win at Dice," which

14

has unfortunately not survived. The extent of his passion for gaming may be deduced from a feature of his traveling chariot, a specially constructed board stabilized for play on the roughest rural roads of the empire. He is said to have wagered 400,000 sesterces, a fortune even by regal standards, on a single roll of the dice. For this indiscretion Seneca relegates the emperor to a Sisyphean gamester's hell: condemned eternally to pick up the bones and throw them into a dice cup that has no bottom.

THE ORIGINS OF DICE

GOD INVENTED DICE. So says Plato, who attributes their conception to the Egyptian deity Theuth. Another tale touts Palamedes, the Greek hero of the Trojan War. His sagacity was legendary, and he is said to have invented such diurnal necessities as dice and eating at regular intervals. He encouraged soldiers to relieve the boredom of the siege of Troy by dicing. Herodotus attributes the discovery of dice to the practical Lydians. To palliate widespread famine, they would eat only every other day and gamble on the fast days.

Almost all early civilizations were interested in chance and divination, a formidable combination that paved the way for high-stakes gambling and philosophical rumination. The direct precursors of dice are astragali, the heel bones of hoofed quadrupeds, which articulate with the tibia and help form the ankle joint. They exhibit a natural symmetry. They are six-sided, with four flat sides; the flat sides alone seem to have been used for gaming. They acquire a natural high polish through handling and are also well suited to decoration. Astragali were used in board games of the Egyptians perhaps as early as 3500 B. C. E. (The *Encyclopedia Britannica* tells us that loaded dice were found in ancient Egyptian tombs.) While sheep were the most common providers of these gaming implements, the astragali of antelope were prized for their elegance. These bones were also used for a fortune-telling divination called astragalomancy. The transition from mammalian heel bones to dice is thought to have been a gradual one.

THE BROKEN DICE

OLAF HARALDSSON, an eleventh-century king of Norway, metamorphosed from a Viking warrior into a Christian saint. Dubbed Olaf the Thick (a characterization based on corpulence rather than lack of cunning), he wagered a kingdom in a game of dice. Not even the healing waters that were said to spout from his grave can match the miraculous tale of the broken dice. King Olaf and the king of Sweden were gambling over competing claims to the island of Hising. The Swede rolled the highest possible score, two sixes, and arrogantly suggested that there was no need for Olaf to take his turn. "Although these be two sixes on the dice, it would be easy, sire, for God to let them turn up again in my favor!" Olaf insisted, basking in the self-confidence of his recent conversion. He then cast two sixes. The Swede again threw two sixes, and so, again, did Olaf—but at the end of this roll, one of the dice split in two, and *both* a six and an ace landed face up, yielding an unprecedented roll of thirteen.

THE TRUE
PRACTICE OF FALSEHOOD

In the early modern period, gambling was often studied in unexpected proximity to apparently higher pursuits. *Toxophilus,* the famous 1544 treatise on archery by Roger Ascham, who was the classics consultant to the Tudor monarchs, is the improbable source of the earliest serious discussion on false dice in English. Ascham enumerates a variety of ways in which a cheater may alter the dice to his advantage, and documents a diabolical scam: If a pigeon is winning honestly, a crook switches false dice into the game. The honest player unwittingly throws them, and another crook accuses the mark of cheating.

A more conscientious discussion of the methods and language of the dice hustler appears in *A Manifest Detection of the Most Vile and Detestable Use of Dice-play,* issued about 1552 and attributed to a Gilbert Walker, about whom nothing is known. The advantageous alteration of dice is analyzed in fourteen exotic variants, couched in the canting language of cheaters: A hustler's kit could include a bale or two of fulhams, high men, low men, "gourds," "light graviers," "demies," or "contraries." "Bristle dice," which were affixed with boar's hair, became too well known "to get the money," or as Walker puts it, were "now too gross a practice to be put in use."

Dicing was virtually synonymous with cheating. In his *Notable Discovery of Coosnage* (1591), Robert Greene, the colorful Elizabethan pamphleteer who called Shakespeare an "upstart crow" and expired ignominiously from a surfeit of pickled herring, defined Cheating Law as "play at false dice." Thomas Dekker's *The Bellman of London* (1608) proffered, "Of all which *Lawes,* the *Highest* in place, and the *Highest* in perdition is the *Cheating Law* or the art of winning money by false dyce."

In *The Last Will and Testament of Laurence Lucifer,* Thomas Middleton bequeathed to "Francis Finger-false, Deputy of Dicing-houses, all cunning lifts, shifts and couches, that ever were, are, and shall be invented, from

this hour of eleven o'clock upon Black Monday, until it smite twelve o'clock at doomsday!" The thief's livelihood would thereby be assured: "If you . . . will truly practice falsely, you may live more gallanter far upon three dice, than many of your foolish heirs about London upon their hundred acres."

Charles Cotton is less well known for *The Compleat Gamester* (1674) than for his contributions to the more pastoral *The Compleat Angler* of Izaak Walton, but he was a serious student of gambling. He mentions a devastating collaboration between a box keeper, the fellow who managed play at an eating house, and a "rook," or hustler, who would fleece the customers using dice provided by the restaurateur. Cotton describes gaffing the cup or box from which the cubes are thrown, and even suggests a test to ensure that the dice are not loaded: Gently hold a die by two corners between your thumb and forefinger, and if, in this delicate grip, they start to rotate, "you may then conclude them false." A more destructive but infallible method is also suggested: "you may try their falsehood otherwise by breaking or splitting them."

In the fourth volume of *The English Rogue* (1680), Richard Head (or more likely his exploitive publisher Francis Kirkman) warns that a gamester taking up dice had best wield his sword, "for should you play upon the Square, you will be suspected by those that loose, you have knapt or put the change of the Dice upon them." The morning after the game played honestly, "you will be scorn'd and slighted, and at last pist on as you walk the streets." A similar sentiment was expressed by my grandfather, who told me when I was a youngster that he never played cards because if he lost he was thought an incompetent magician and if he won he was suspected a cheater.

FACT AND FICTION

THE DISPARATE WORLDS OF science and literature are both replete with references to dicing. Aristotle's students, who published *Problematica* in the first century C.E., included two queries on loaded dice. More importantly, modern research on probability originated in the analysis of games of chance with dice. Among the remarkable mathematicians interested in the cubes were Cardano, Galileo, Fermat, Pascal, and De Moivre.

The backbone of Indian literature is the epic poem *The Mahabarata,* in which the fate of battling families turns on the roll of false dice. In the

West, the rogue tradition is represented in the works of Villon, Rabelais, and Cervantes, who frequently dip into the idiom of the swindler and the world of the cheat. In Germany the source of such material is the *Liber Vagatorum,* which features the "Rothwelsch," or beggar's lingo. Inspired by these sources, Hans Jakob Christoffel von Grimmelshausen wrote the Simplician Cycle, the most important German fiction of the seventeenth century. *Simplicissimus the Vagabond* contains a chapter on dice play in a battlefield, executed in an area almost as large as the market square in the center of Cologne. The players divided into groups, each of which, according to the translation of John Osborne, "had a trafficker-in-vice — I meant to say 'trafficker-in-dice,' though dice do hold their prey as fast as in a vise." These traffickers, who supplied the gaming equipment, were supposed to ensure that no cheating took place, but a metamorphic array of false dice were switched into the game. Among them were "Dutch ones, which must be rolled so that they skitter along the table; they had two fives, on opposite sides, and two sixes, and were as sharp-ridged as the skinny mules they give soldiers to ride. Other dice were high German ones; these you must hold as high as the Bavarian Alps when you are about to toss them. Some were made of hartshorn, light on top and heavy on the bottom; others were loaded with quicksilver or lead, and yet others had sharp edges; on the others the edges were filed off completely; some were long and club-shaped; and some looked like fat toads. And all of these sorts of dice were made for the sole purpose of cheating." When these dice were discovered, they were smashed or bitten in half by irate gamesters.

MATTHEW BUCHINGER

Sᴏᴍᴇᴛɪᴍᴇs ᴛʜᴇ ᴍᴀɴ rather than the dice was disfigured, as in the case of Matthew Buchinger, born in Germany in 1674. The "Little Man of Nuremberg" was only twenty-nine inches tall and had no arms or legs but was blessed with remarkable skills. With his stumps he performed a variety of conjuring effects, played musical instruments, and produced miniature calligraphy.

His prowess at manipulating the bones undetected is recorded in a broadside from 1726 entitled *A Poem on Mathew Buckinger, The Greatest German Living*:

He throws the Dice as careless down
As any Gamester in the Town.
And tho' the Number cast be three
Two Sixes you shall ever see.

THE PALINGENESIS OF CRAPS

Acording to an opuscule of this felicitous title penned by Edward Larocque Tinker and published by the Press of the Woolly Whale in 1933, the game of craps owes its etymology to a racial slur. The game was introduced in America in the early nineteenth century by Bernard Xavier Philippe de Marigny de Mandeville, a New Orleans native who while traveling in London learned the pleasures of the dicing recreation known as hazard from the sporting set called "the fancy." The entertainment became so popular among the Creoles of New Orleans that visitors from the North referred to it disparagingly as "Johnny Crapaud's game"—having first designated the French-Americans "Johnny Crapauds," a pejorative term based on their reputed propensity for supping on frogs. The diminutive "craps" was soon in vogue. For more than fifty years New Orleans boasted a *rue de Craps,* an homage coined by Marigny to commemorate his enormous losses at the game he championed.

It is prudent to add that this tale has been dismissed as apocryphal by historians of gaming, and ignored entirely by the *Oxford English Dictionary.* The second edition of the *OED* insists on the term's "obscure origins," favoring the simpler explanation that craps is a corruption of *crabs,* a slang designation for a pair of ones in the venerable game of hazard.

The modern rules of craps: A player rolls two dice. If they total seven or eleven he wins; if two, three, or twelve he loses. Any other total rolled is called his "point," and he must then try to throw for his point. If he rolls his point before seven comes up, he wins; if seven comes up first, he loses.

The Litany of a Craps Dealer

"Ladies and Gentleman get your money down it's betting time. The hard six and the hard eight gets you 7 to 1. The hard ten, the hard four gets you 8 to 1. I repeat, get your money down it's betting time and we're off...

Comin' out for a point. Bet the big eleven. Seven is a crap. Bet the field. They come or they don't come. Five and after five, the field, they come or they don't come. Leave your money set and win a big bet. Don't cut it thin you won't win. Leave it go — watch it grow.

And the winner five on the front line.

And we're comin' out for another point, e-o-lev, the winner."

THE PRICE OF DICE

The use of illicit dice might seem an inevitability more than a temptation; nonetheless the punishments were often severe and could be harder on the manufacturers than the players.

In the thirteenth century, the German legal compendium known as the Mirror of Saxony recorded that citizens possessing false dice were publicly scourged. Those caught using false dice had their hands cut off, and those who fabricated false dice, considered the greatest offenders, had their eyes put out so they could never make such offending objects again.

In England there are court records citing the prosecution of men for using doctored dice as early as the fourteenth century. One convicted man was forced to endure the indignity of the pillory with his false dice strung about his neck. Nonetheless, the manufacture of false dice was so prevalent by 1598 that Queen Elizabeth ordered a search and seizure warrant, "forasmuch as great abuse hath bene comytted and daily is committed by the making of false dice and dyce of advantage and by reason thereof by playne Cosenage and deceipt manie of her Majesties subjects stripped of their goodes and patrimony."

As a result of this enforcement, perhaps, false dice flourished in prisons. Geffray Mynshul noted in 1618 that one could learn more about rogueries in jail than in twenty dicing houses. A half-century earlier Gilbert Walker announced that false dice could be readily obtained in the prisons of Marshalsea or King's Bench. The labor of good professionals, though, was always at a premium. Walker extolled the workmanship of Bird of Holborn, the first such craftsman known by name. In *The Compleat Gamester,* Cotton mentions that a bale of dice loaded with quicksilver was readily available for eight shillings, while a non-gaffed bale could be obtained for only sixpence. Poor manufacture was easily

detected. According to the anonymous author of *The Whole Art and Mystery of Modern Gaming fully Expos'd and Detected* (London, 1726), shaved dice were "made always proportionable to the Impudence of the Operator; for you must know, there are some made so very strong, that you may discover them as soon as put upon the Table; a modest Man takes more Caution."

In France during the reign of Henry IV, the court was in the midst of a veritable gambling craze, and an Italian advantage player named Pilmentel enjoyed great success. It was rumored that Pilmentel's good fortune was sanctioned at the highest level, the king believing that the impoverishment of his courtiers strengthened the monarchy. Pilmentel managed to purchase the entire stock of dice in Paris, and he then had an accomplice provide a new shipment at unusually low prices. The merchants and eventually the gamesters who purchased the dice became unwitting accomplices of the Italian: they did not realize that every cube was doctored to his specifications. There was barely a game in Paris that did not play into the hands of this *Chevalier d'Industrie*.

Such objects of deception are still offered for sale, often under the guise of conjuring supplies sold "for entertainment purposes only." A handyman hustler in the 1940s did not have to rely on shop-crafted wares but could fashion his own false dice with the equipment outlined in a catalog issued by a Los Angeles firm:

We are supplying a Special Selected Outfit that is complete for those wishing to do their own work. The outfit consists of one hand drill, one vise, four sizes of straight drills, three burrs for hollowing, celluloid rope for plugging, one bottle of cement, white and black dice ink, one box of amalgam, one bottle of mercury, four finishing drills for spots, adjustable spot spacer, polishing compound, fast cutting sand for shaping and corner work, file, sample of three dice, drilled and hollowed to show just how work should be done for perfect balance. Instruction with each item to show best way to handle.

Dice Makers Outfit, complete $18.00

DICE AND DEITY

GOD KILLS WITH DICE. In 1714 Theofiles Lucas related the tale of three Swiss gamesters who defy God. They are playing on the Sabbath. As one man casts the dice he exclaims that if fortune failed him he "would thrust his Dagger into the very Body of God, as far as he could." Upon losing his throw he hurls his dirk toward the heavens. The dagger disappears in midair and three drops of blood land on the table in front of the frightened gamblers. For this blasphemy, the devil instantly carries the wretch away, "with such a noise and stink that the whole city was amazed at it." The townspeople capture and enchain another of the dicers, who is suddenly struck dead en route to the prison. The third is put to death by the citizens, who make a monument of the gaming table as an object lesson on the evils of gambling and the judgment of God.

Sacrilege also proved fatal in the case of a Florentine nobleman, Antonio Rinaldeschi. In 1501 he wagered and lost a considerable sum on a roll of the dice. According to the aghast witnesses, he stood up, cursed the name of the Virgin, and departed the Fig Tree Tavern; then, passing the church of S. Maria de'Ricci, he stooped and picked up a handful of dry horse dung, which he hurled at a fresco of the Madonna. The missile remained affixed to the effigy just above the nape of her neck. The resulting outcry anticipated by five hundred years the furor surrounding the exhibition of Chris Ofili's *Holy Virgin Mary,* which featured a black Madonna with breasts rendered from dry elephant dung. A major protest greeted the show in which it appeared — "Sensation," at the Brooklyn Museum — but the fate of that artist was not as dire as that of Rinaldeschi. When the Florentine was apprehended, according to an article by William J. Connel and Giles Constable, he tried to commit suicide by stabbing himself with a dagger. The gamester, however, survived his own attack. In protective custody he was escorted away from a lynch mob. He confessed, both to a magistrate and a priest, received absolution, and later the same evening was hanged.

The Universal Baseball Association, Inc., J. Henry Waugh, Prop., Robert Coover's aleatory novel, features a benign and hopelessly neurotic twentieth-century god. J. Henry Waugh (read *Yahweh*) is a middle-aged accountant obsessed with the baseball league he has created. His game is played by rolling three dice and comparing the casts to an elaborate series of tables and contingency charts. He pauses only to gulp pastrami sandwiches and release his tension with an aging "B" girl, increasingly forsaking his friends and his job to roll the dice, hour after hour, day after day. Onomastically selecting patronymics and monikers, obsessively recording not only earned run averages, strikeouts, and stolen bases but also every detail of the players' existence, he creates a book of life. He suffers a nervous break-down after one odds-defying roll causes the death of his greatest player.

DICE AND DEATH

IN THE FIRST CENTURY, Tacitus writes that among the Germanic hordes men earned their destinies as slaves or free men by throwing the bones. An illustration in a fourteenth-century manuscript reveals two dicers, one reduced to his shirt and the other completely unclothed, in an early version of strip dice. In an example of rough justice from ancient Persia, a woman wagers against the king for the life of a subject. After a favorable roll she claims her prize and then has him put to death for having decapitated her son.

The tales of gamblers driven to suicide by bad fortune at dice are legion. The Rev. Charles Caleb Colton writes in *Lacon, or many Things in few Words addressed to those who think* (1820), "The gamester, if he die a martyr to his profession, is doubly ruined. He adds his soul to every other loss, and by the act of suicide renounces earth to forfeit heaven." This very Colton, whose book was an unprecedented literary success, who was far more renowned as a gambler than as a divine (he is said to have won and eventually lost 25,000 pounds in the gambling salons of the Palais Royal), took his own life.

WHEN A DIE DIES

In the attempt to acquire empirical knowledge, I have accumulated thousands of dice over a period of decades. They are of myriad size, shape, and color and of daunting variety: birdseye, bullseye, doughnut, barbudi, poker, baseball, golf, crown and anchor, bell and hammer, drugstore, razor, brushed, feathered, juice, weight, hits, missouts, tops, shapes, polyhedrons, teetotums, and rough-cut unnumbered cubes. They come from diverse sources: generous friends, dealers in collectibles, distraught gamblers ready to embrace a new calling. They are fabricated from different materials, but the vast majority are made of celluloid.

In 1868 John Wesley Hyatt formed a substance from a homogeneous colloidal dispersion of nitric acid, sulphuric acid, cotton fibers, and camphor. It was a substance of great tensile strength capable of resisting the effects of water, oils, and even diluted acids. Hyatt's brother called it celluloid, and it became the first commercially successful synthetic plastic. It was cost-effective to manufacture and could be produced in a variety of attractive colors. Heated until soft and molded into shapes, it became a substitute for products fashioned out of ivory, tortoiseshell, and horn. Perhaps it is best known for its use in motion-picture film, where its volatility has resulted in the destruction of a vast percentage of early footage. But it was also used to fashion removable collars, collar stays, knife handles, guitar picks, piano keys, billiard balls, and, of course, dice.

These cellulose nitrate dice, the industry standard until the middle of the twentieth century (when they were replaced with less flammable cellulose acetate), typically remain stable for decades. Then, in a flash, they can dramatically decompose. The crystallization begins on the corners and then spreads to the edges. Nitric acid is released in a process called outgassing. The dice cleave, crumble, and then implode. Unpaired electrons or free radicals can abet the deterioration. The light and smog

of Los Angeles, where my dice have resided for many years, are likely accomplices.

To record the death of my dice I called Rosamond Purcell, doyenne of decaying objects, photographer of taxidermological specimens, memorist of *Wunderkammern.* Her studio in Cambridge is bedizened with *objets trouvés* in various stages of decomposition: Rescued sheets of discarded metal and weather-beaten books that are transformed — by design, by vision, by respect — into objects of great beauty. She has come to know my dice, she has scrutinized them. She has analyzed every nuance of shape and color. She has at once halted their disintegration and catalyzed their resurrection. The dice have never looked better.

Afterword

It's a good thing for me and for the camera that Ricky Jay kept his dice. Only a committed archivist would have bothered to keep these particular dice—warped, crumbling, and sometimes smelly—yet stored with care in venerable plastic drawers. I do not fully understand what it is about the visual effects of patina and decay that pushes the button for some of us, but I knew at first glance that the camera would treat each die as one piece of cake after another: delectable abstractions of objects in transition. So fragile I had to use tweezers to lift them, so powdery and odiferous I tried not to inhale their noxious fumes—the precarious condition of the dice enhanced their intrigue.

Manufactured within each type to be as precisely identical as possible, each die has undergone a series of chemical changes and is now an original—one of a kind. No longer significant as numerological devices in a game of chance, the dice are nonetheless still subject to the laws of chance, which drive their individual dramas of volatile decay. Each die, on its inexorable course to extinction, might at any moment go up in smoke or fall apart in the afternoon sun.

⊙ ⊙ ⊙

The only surface of dice in play that matters to the player faces upward. The surfaces of most of these dice are rent by fissures and branching tears; the values (spots or pips) are disoriented, signaling the onset of imploding forces that will in time eradicate all meaning and end in rubble.

The condition of Ricky Jay's dice runs the gamut from near-new to exhaustion. Their opacity ranges from cloudy to transparent. The surfaces of some, once smooth as ivory, have begun to sink and fold inward like lava (p. 25). Others develop a surface powder (p. 37) or overall pattern of fissures before they crumble (p. 53), and still others fall apart into cornices and spikes (p. 61). Now as an X ray, now as a klieg light, the sun illuminates the interiors of the more translucent dice, revealing viscous rooms within mutable walls. I stacked red, orange, and yellow dice on the edge of a balcony, where they glowed like buildings at dusk; I built a tower of yellow dice that gleamed as if under casino lights. The sun came in on all sides, revealing that even these dice were loaded with nothing but trouble. For in the bodies of the most transparent, what looked like ants or spiders preserved as fossils in amber were, in fact, traces and webs of incipient dissolution — the fault lines along which the structure will eventually divide.

I use "spots" to refer to those painted discs on the surface of the dice, "pits" to the painted hollows. As the dice self-destruct, so do the values — spots and pits — but they do so in different ways.

A group of opalescent pinkish dice are filled with cotton, which bulges through the broken sides. The pits on these dice (and on these alone) are warped, squeezed into rough ovals and triangles. Perhaps these shapes under pressure point to some crookedness within (p. 48). On other dice the pits look like eggs, eclipses of the moon, crucibles for green copper gardens (p. 44). A hole can go nowhere but down, although in one group (p. 41) sedimentary slices of pitted dice have detached to float free, holes and all, like Swiss cheese jigsaw pieces.

Most of the pits are subject to the same fate as the surface of the dice, for when decay has reached a hollow, its edges are already abraded, its bottom becomes the top, and that top begins to crumble.

As they disintegrate, the flat spots may be halved, quartered, axed by some cataclysmic tear — white spots may turn tar-black and poisonous crystals and crusts creep across every surface — inorganic putrefaction (p. 12). Yet the spots are more tenacious and mobile than the pits, for when the matrix of the host die compresses, its spots react by sinking in disguise as part-time pits. When that substructure too becomes unstable, they move along, autonomous now, migrating across borders to other dice, slipping round corners, sticking close to fellow spots, towing loads of grime on their tough painted tops.

I observed one of these spots functioning as a last-resort clamp, holding a cornice to an adjacent wall. When the walls of the dice have collapsed altogether, the spots land intact in a pile of glassy shards.

That the spots survive after the dice decay is like an afterimage of their power to make, or break, the gambler.

ROSAMOND PURCELL

Acknowledgments

An act of fate (the unpredictably long run of my show *Ricky Jay: On the Stem* in New York City) has separated me from my library in Los Angeles and from my notes on this monograph. It is my goal to provide a bibliographic essay at a later date. With trepidation at the possibility of oversight or faulty memory, I gratefully acknowledge the help of the following in various and sundry ways: Susan Green, David Roth, Victoria Steele, Dan Chariton, David Singmaster, Harold Cataquet, a slew of helpful folk at the Museum of London, and David Remnick, Cressida Leyshorn, and Anne Stringfield of *The New Yorker* magazine, in which much of the text and several of the photographs originally appeared. Rosamond Purcell adds her thanks to Elisabeth Biondi of *The New Yorker* art department. Collectively, the photographer and author thank: Dennis Purcell, Jim Mairs, Laura Lindgren, Patrick Reagh, Chrisann Verges, Giles Constable, and Lawrence Weschler.